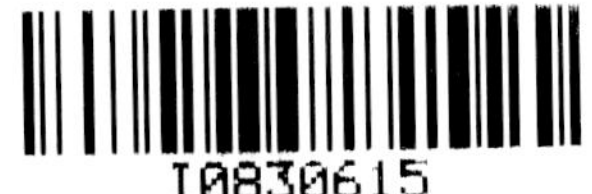

Mellow the F*ck Out

A Coloring Book for Adults

Sutter Holloway

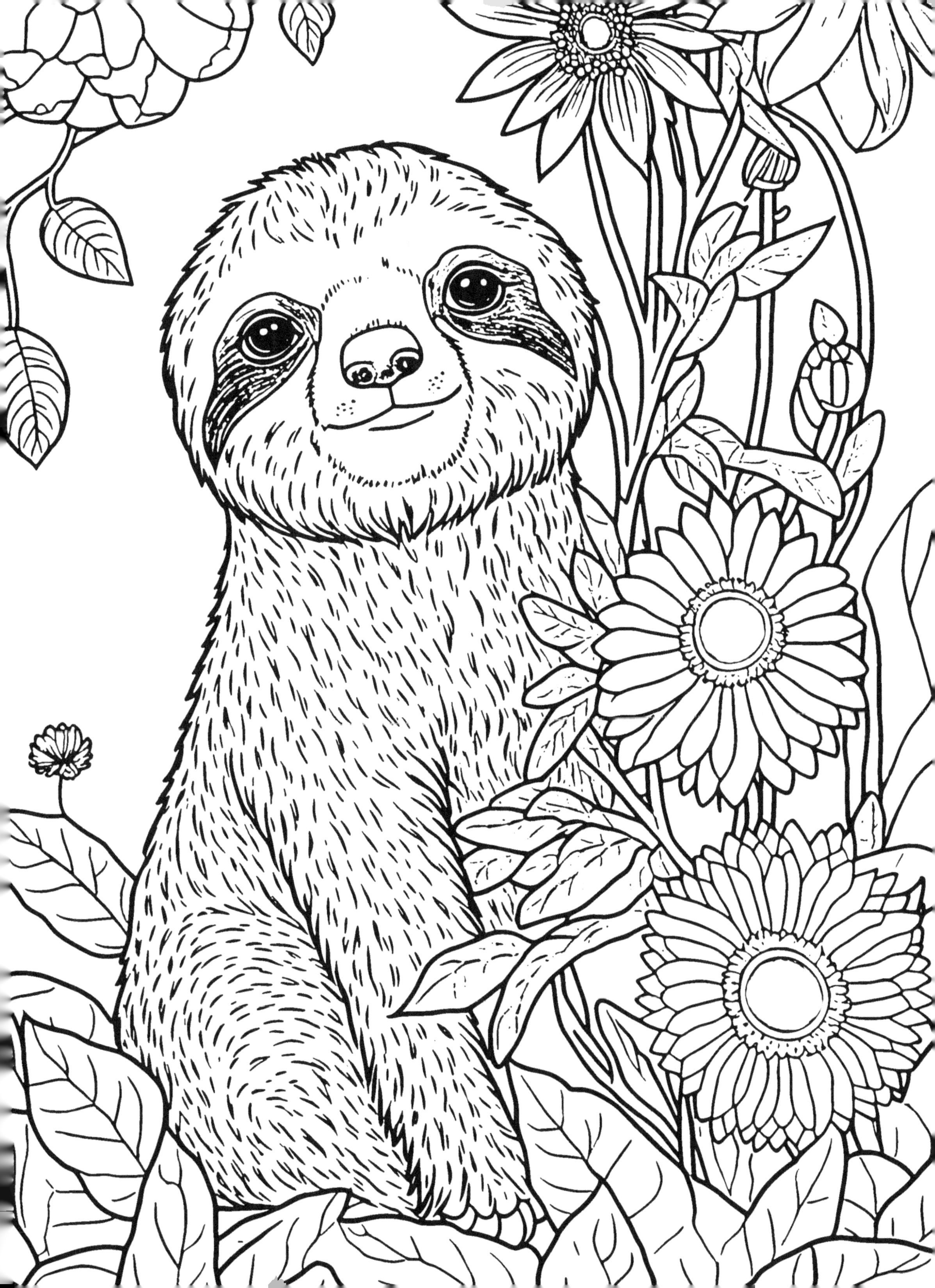

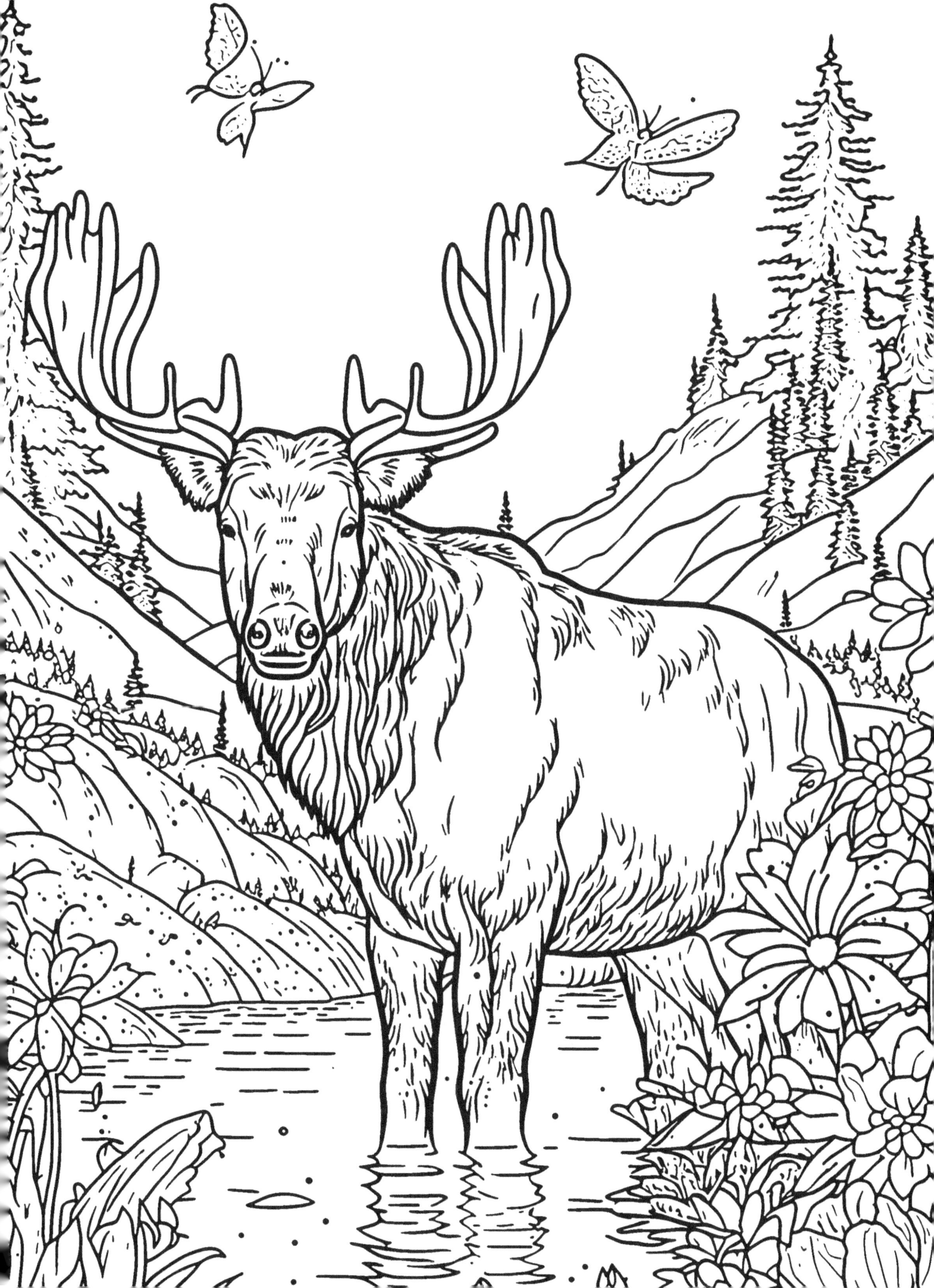

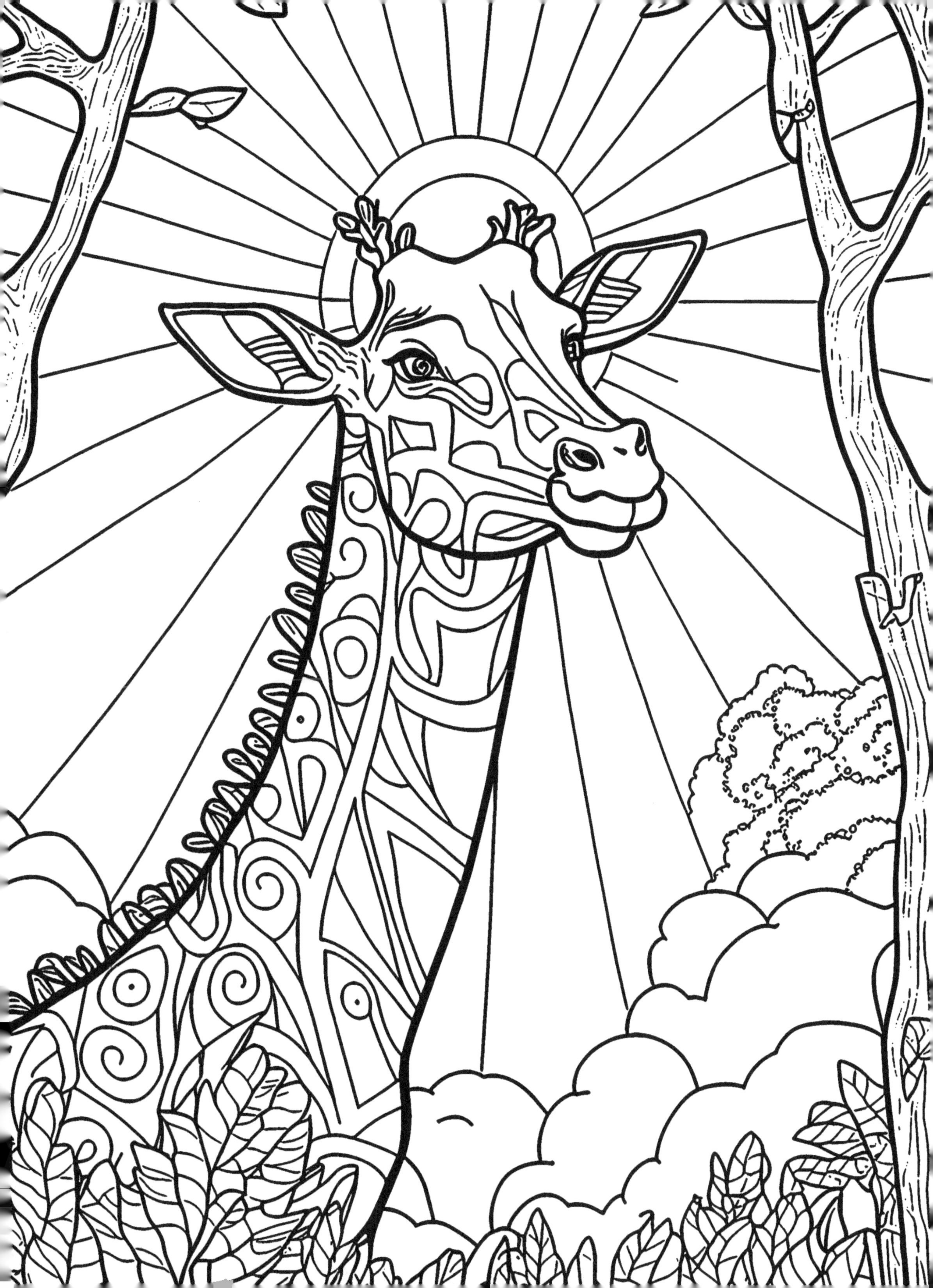

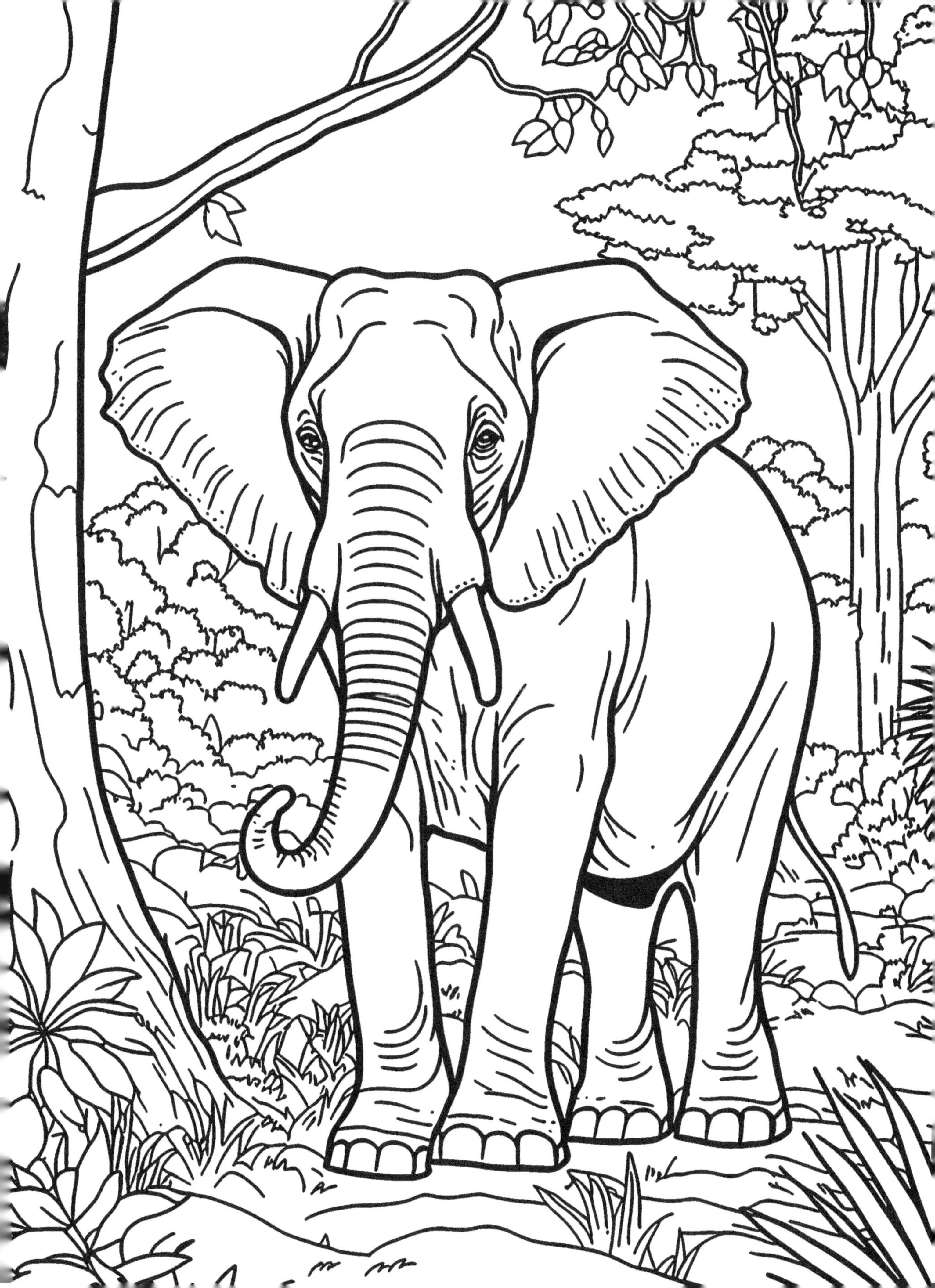

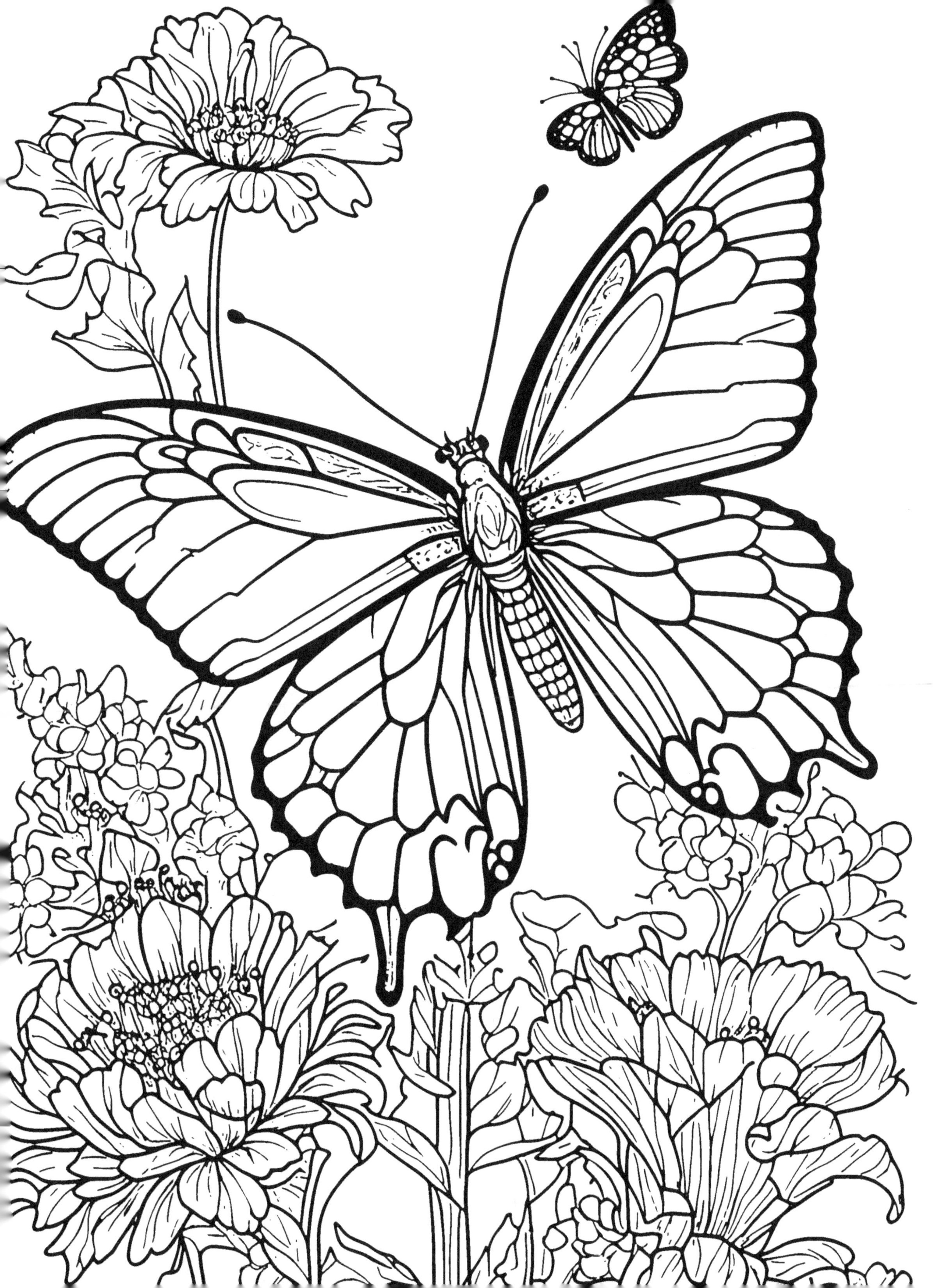

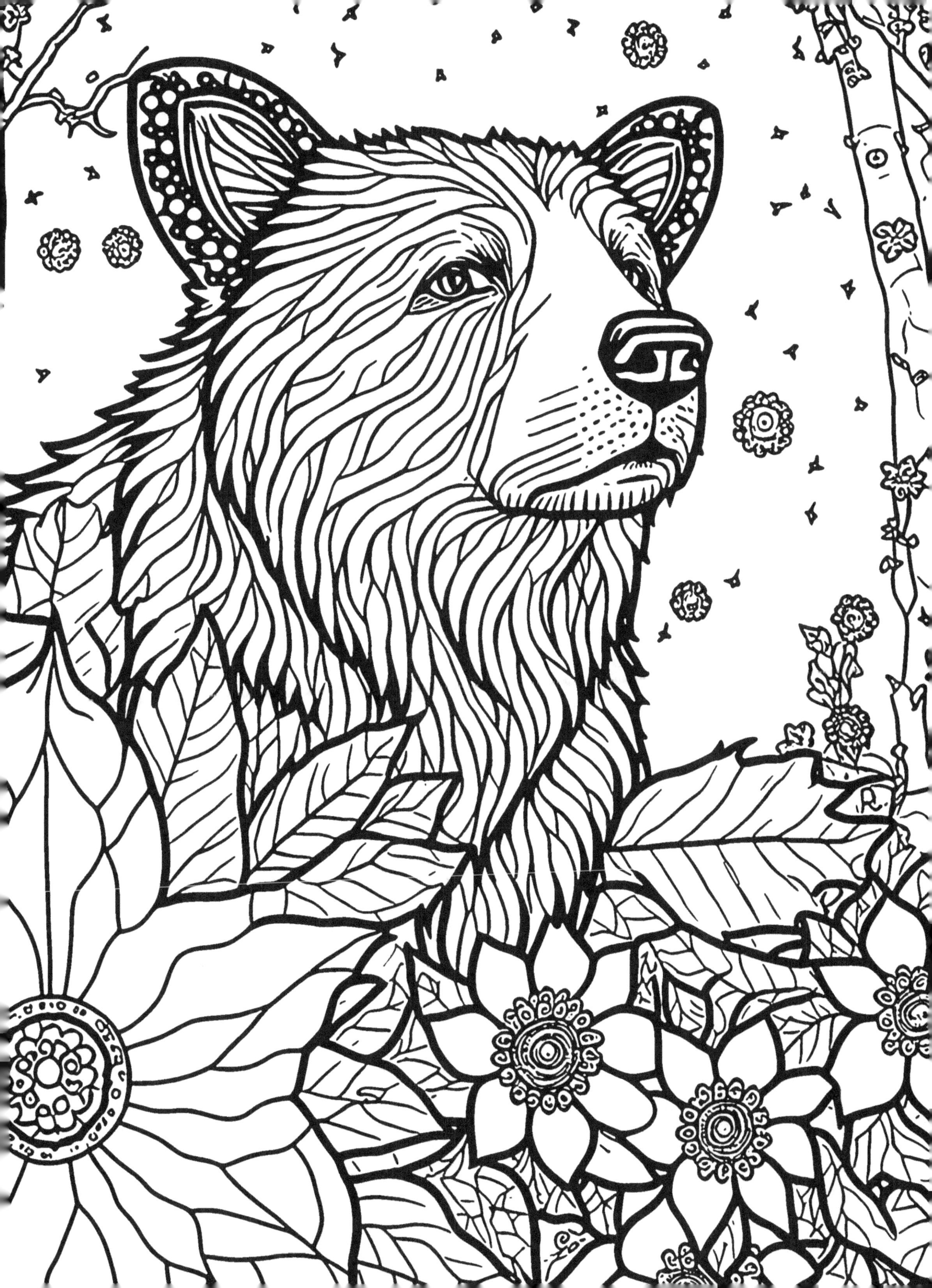

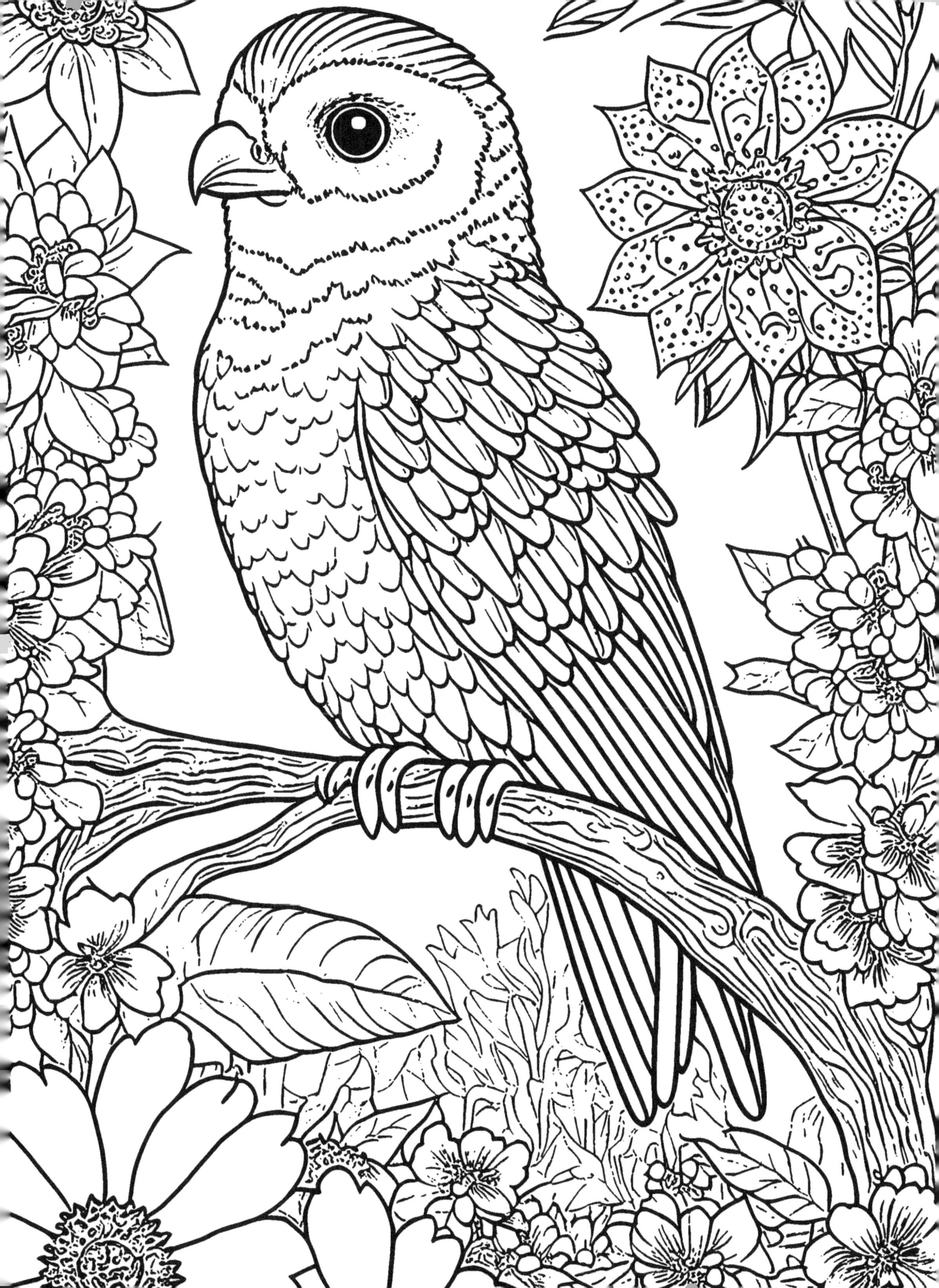

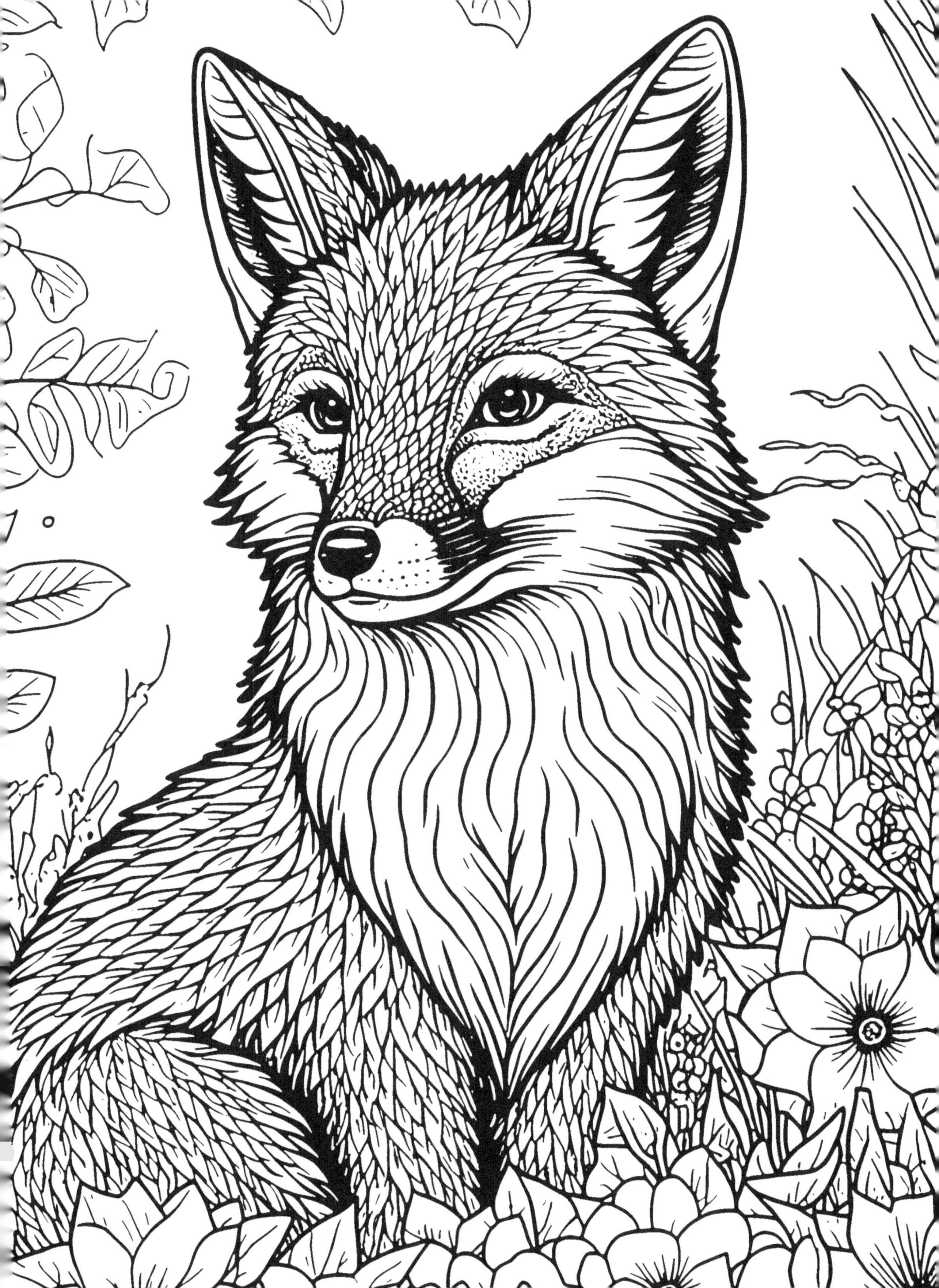

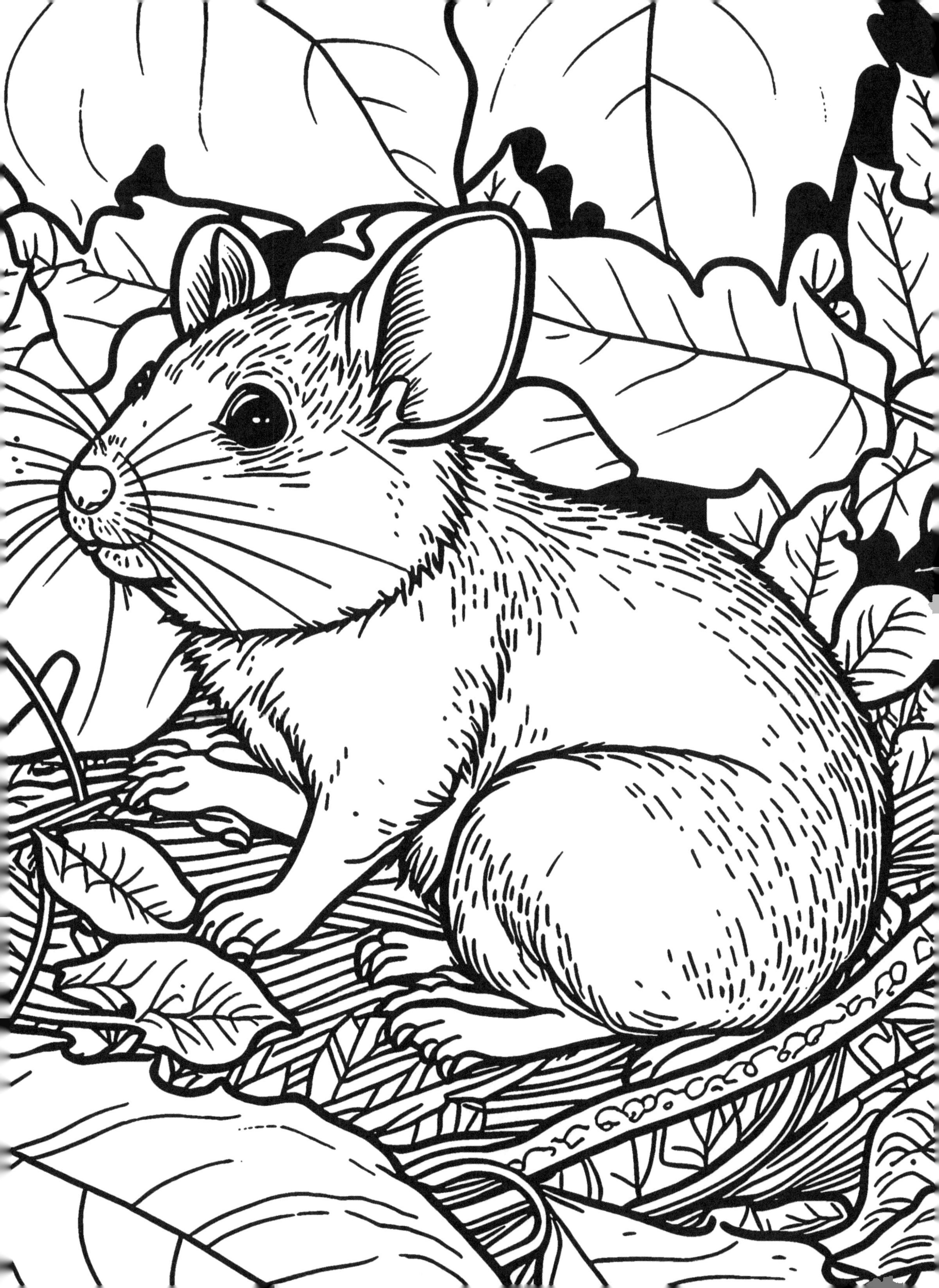

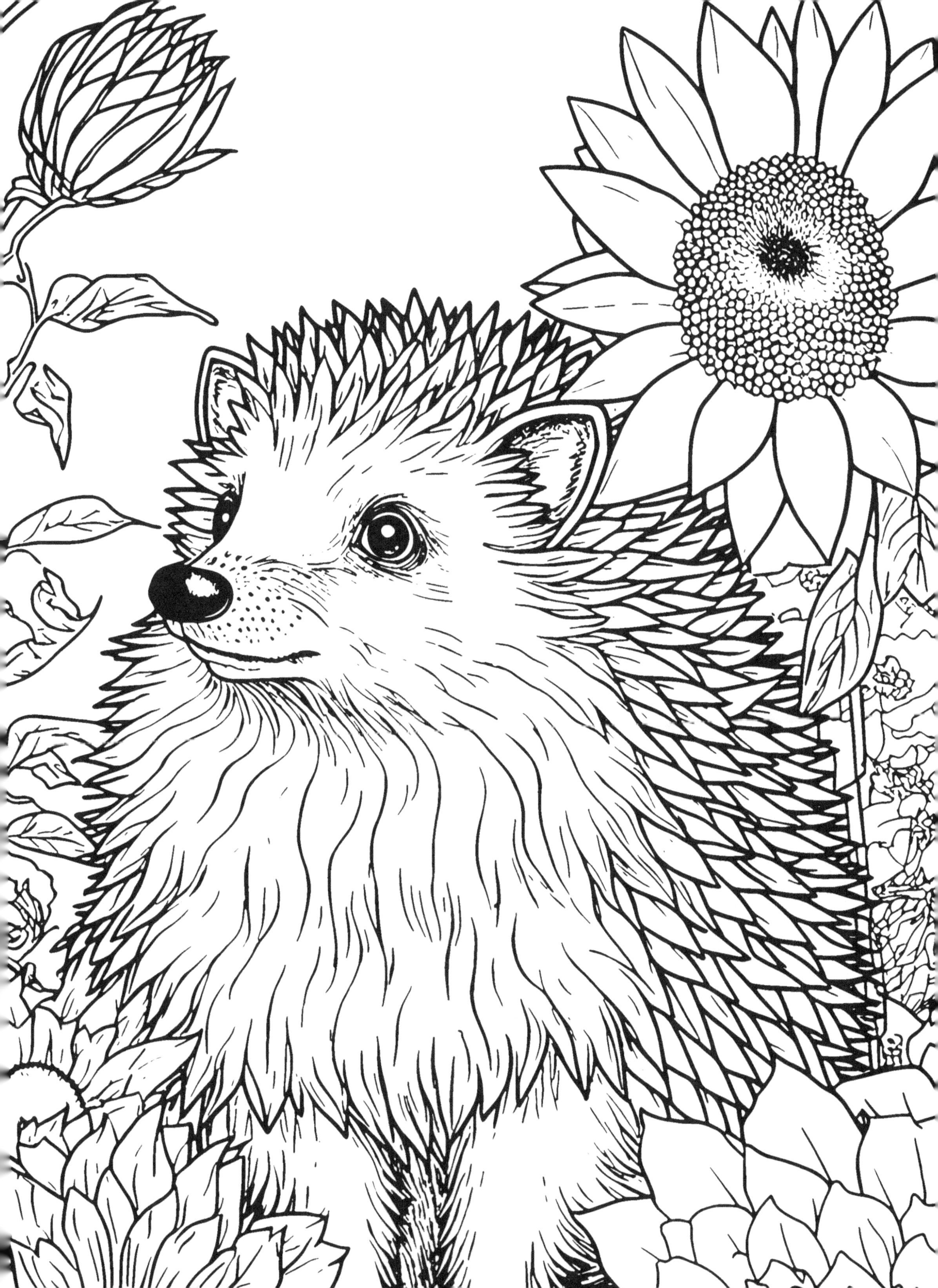

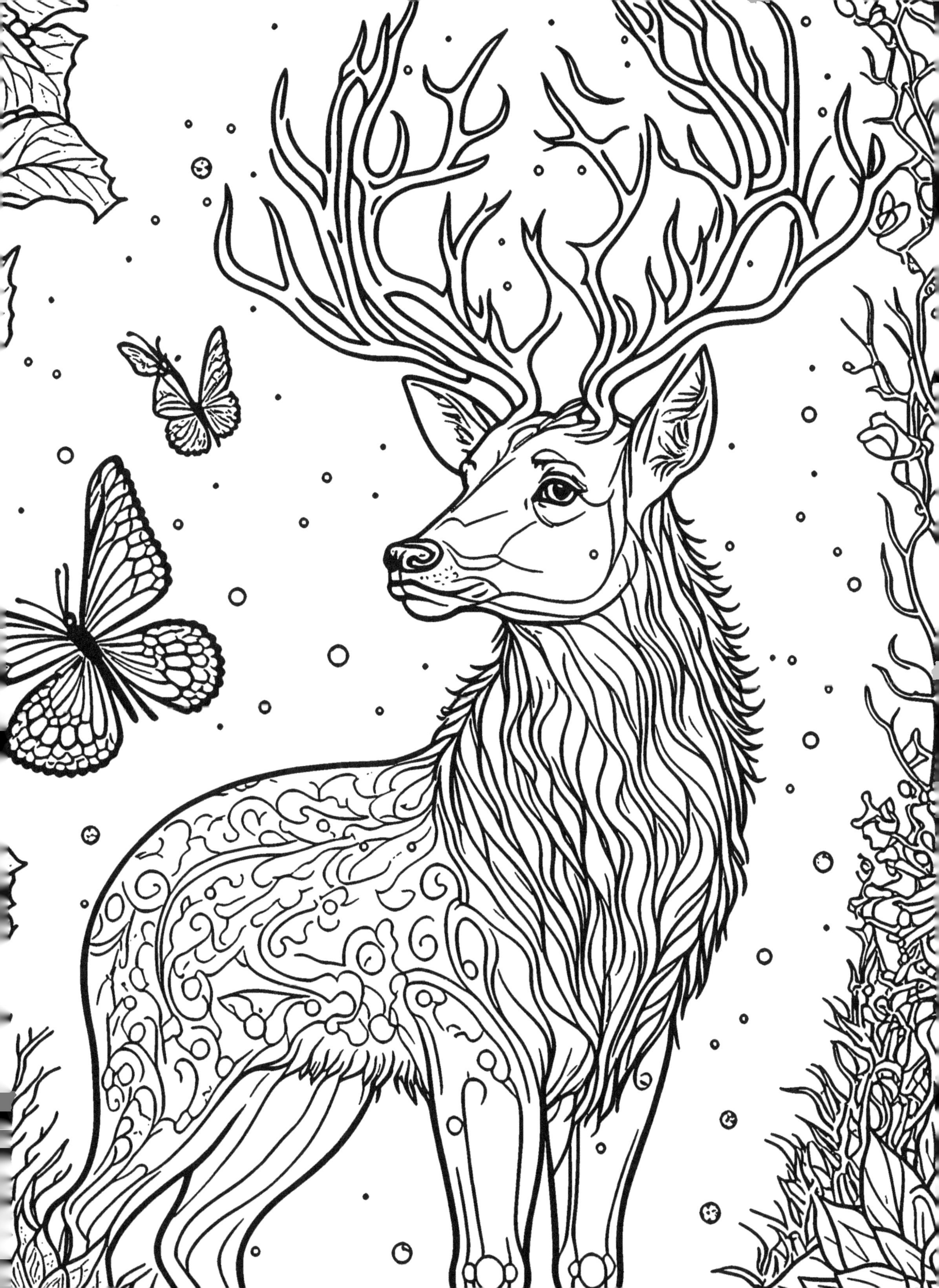

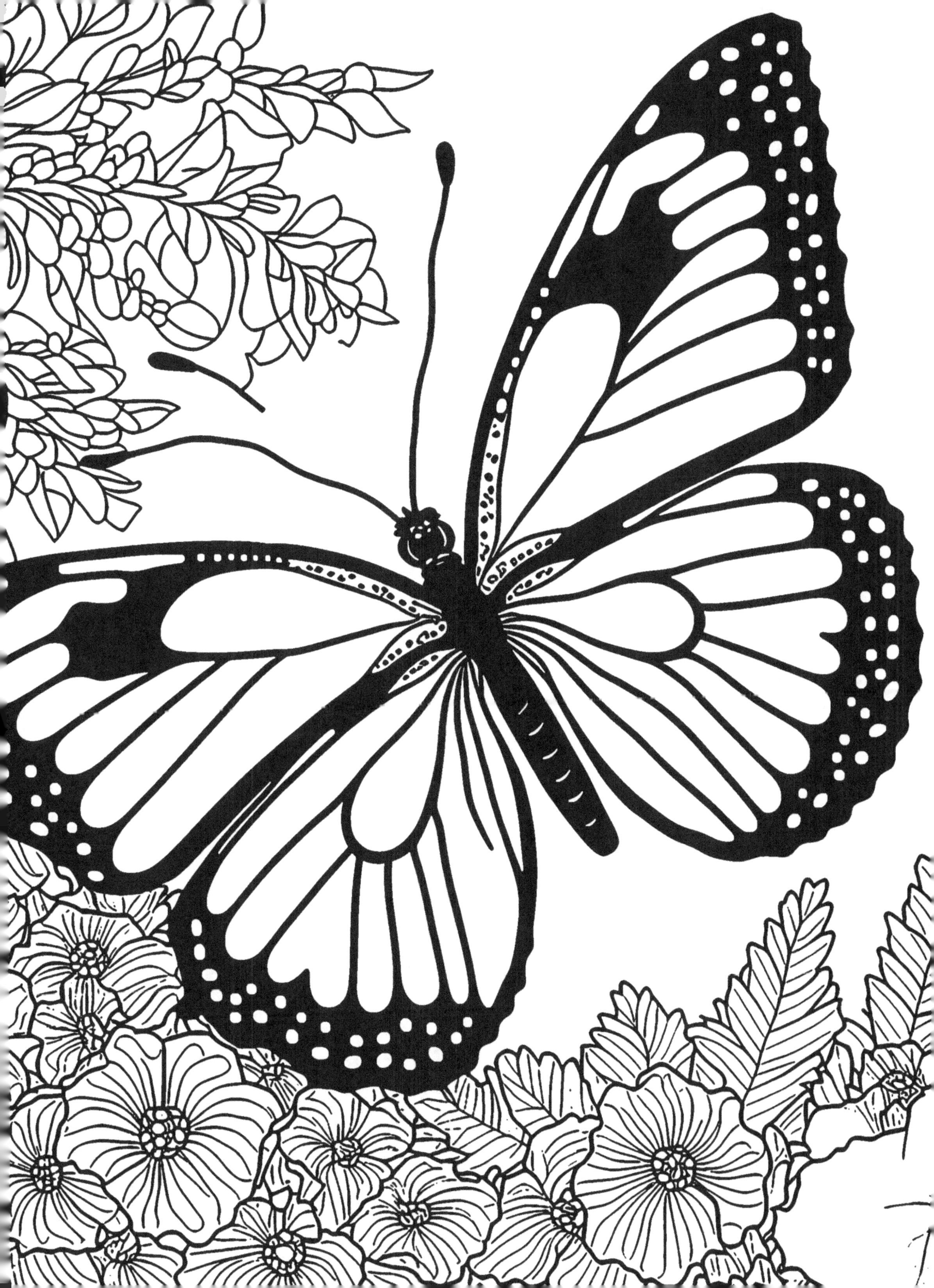

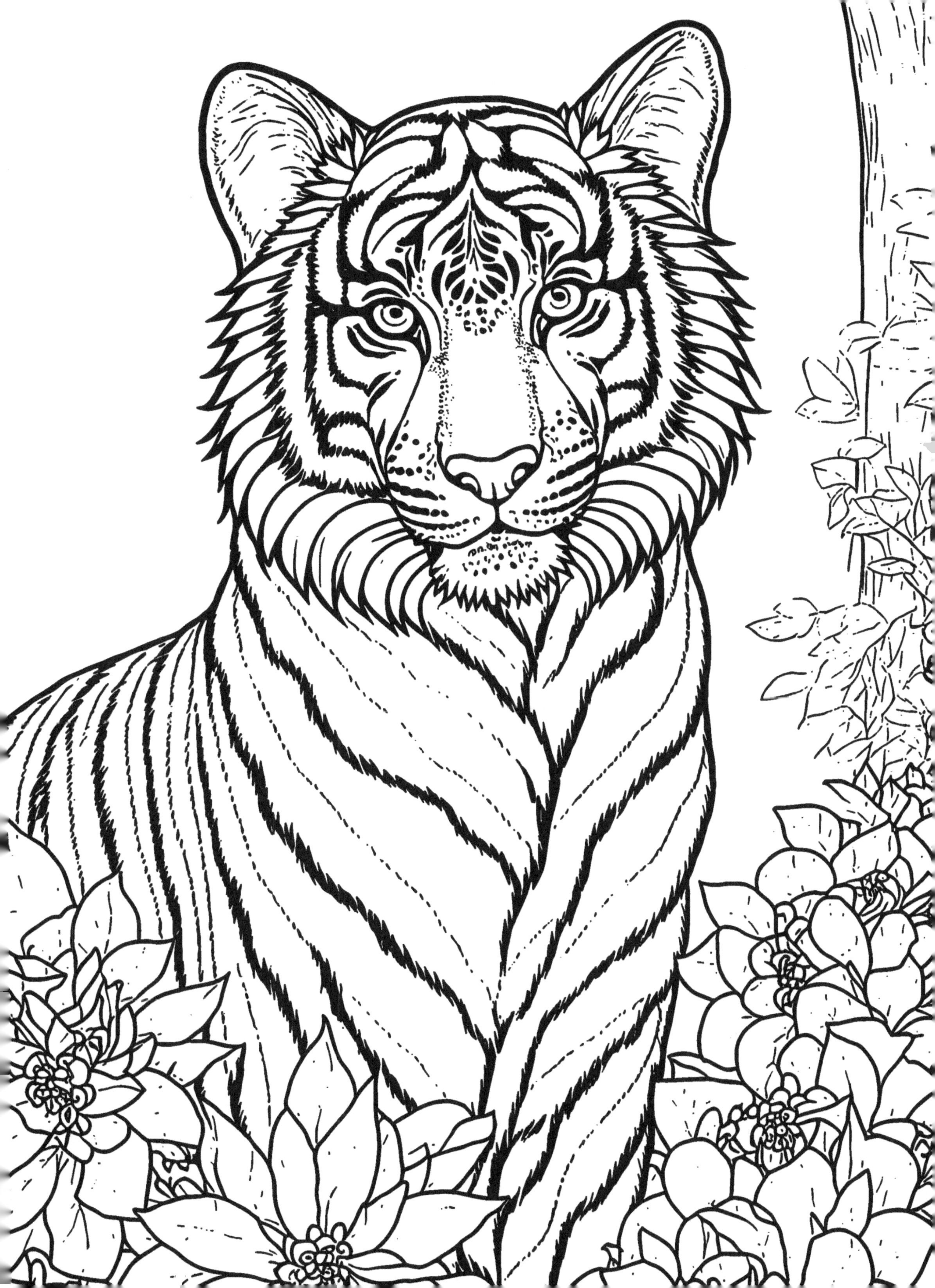

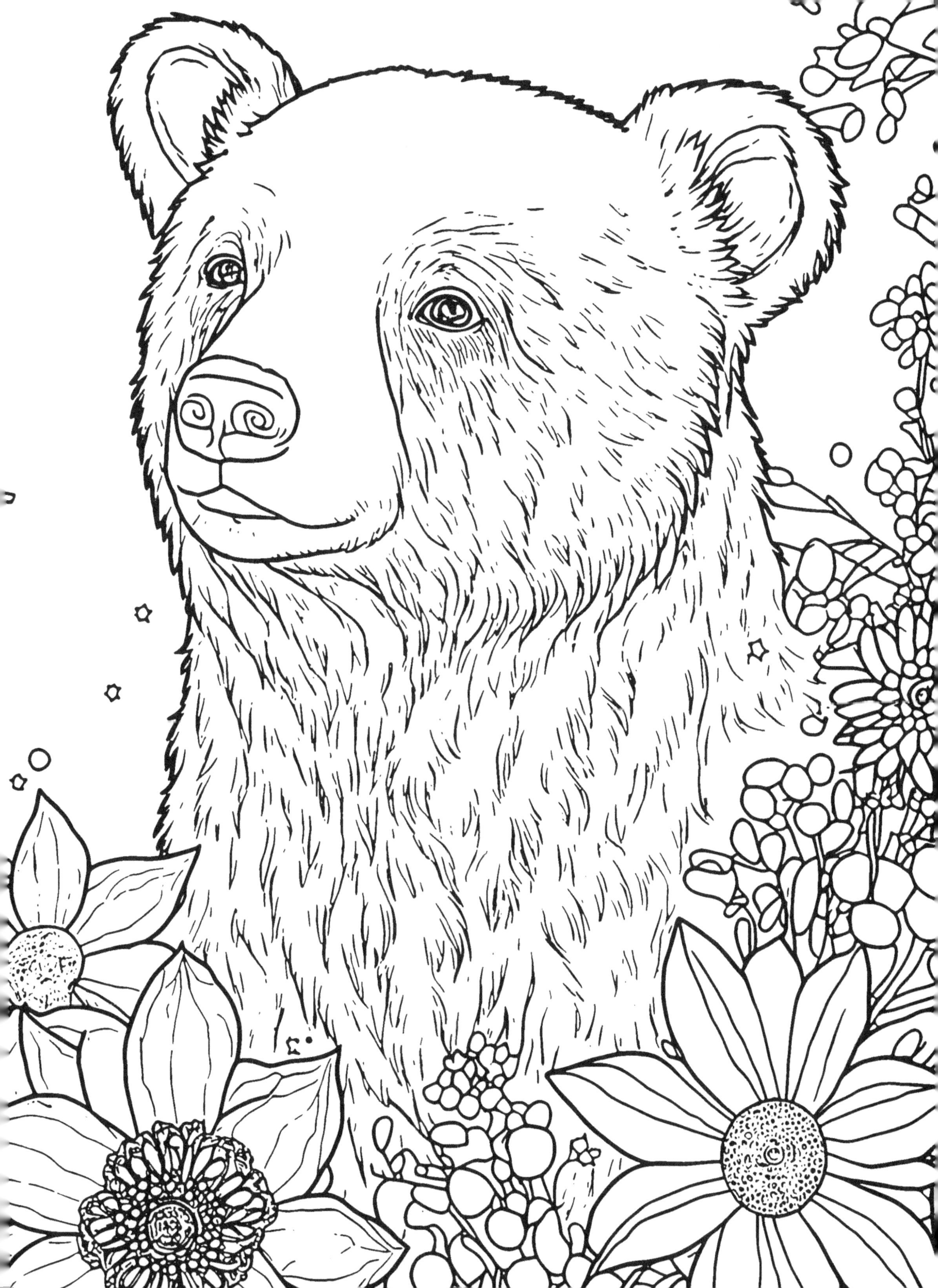

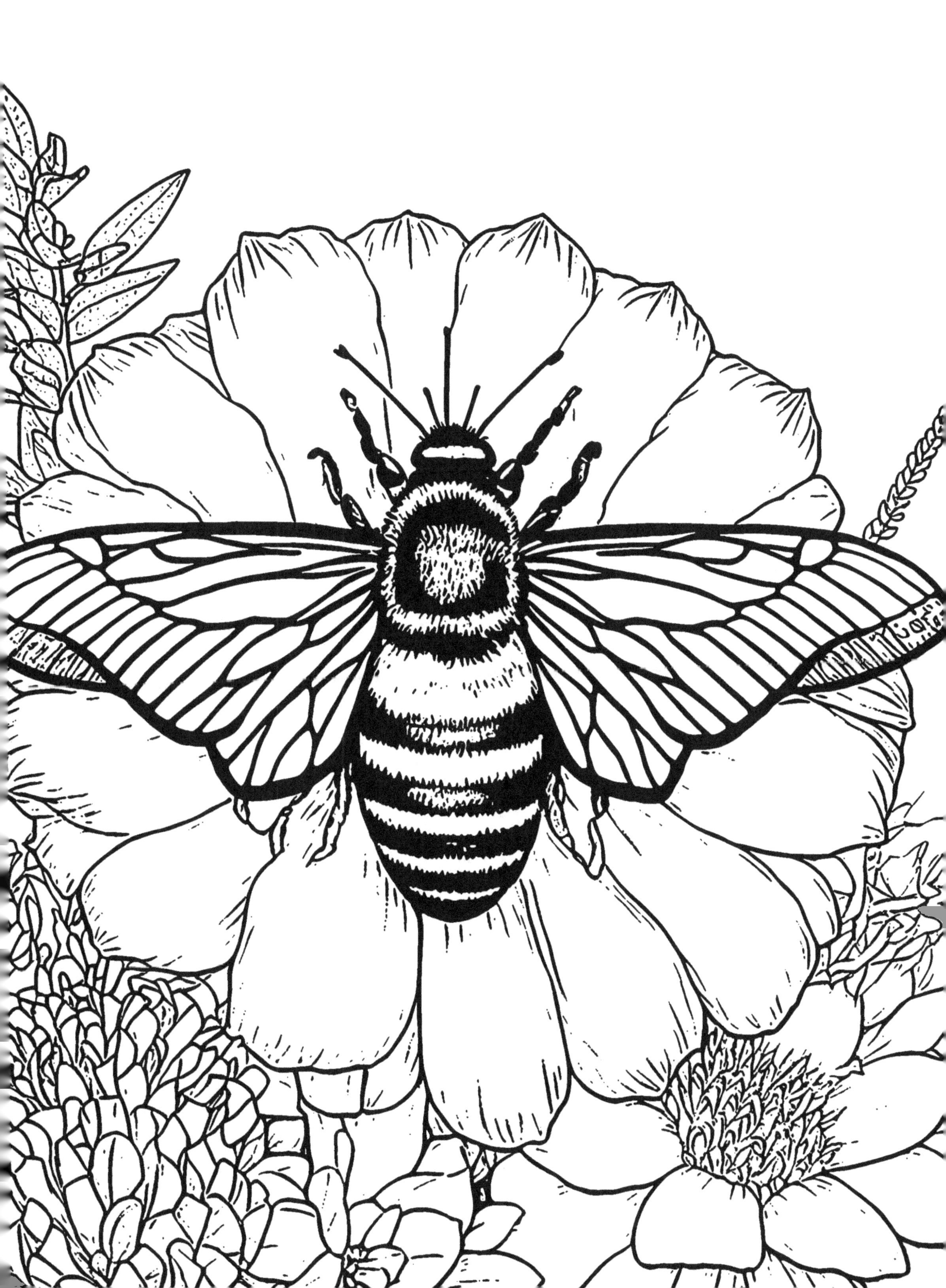

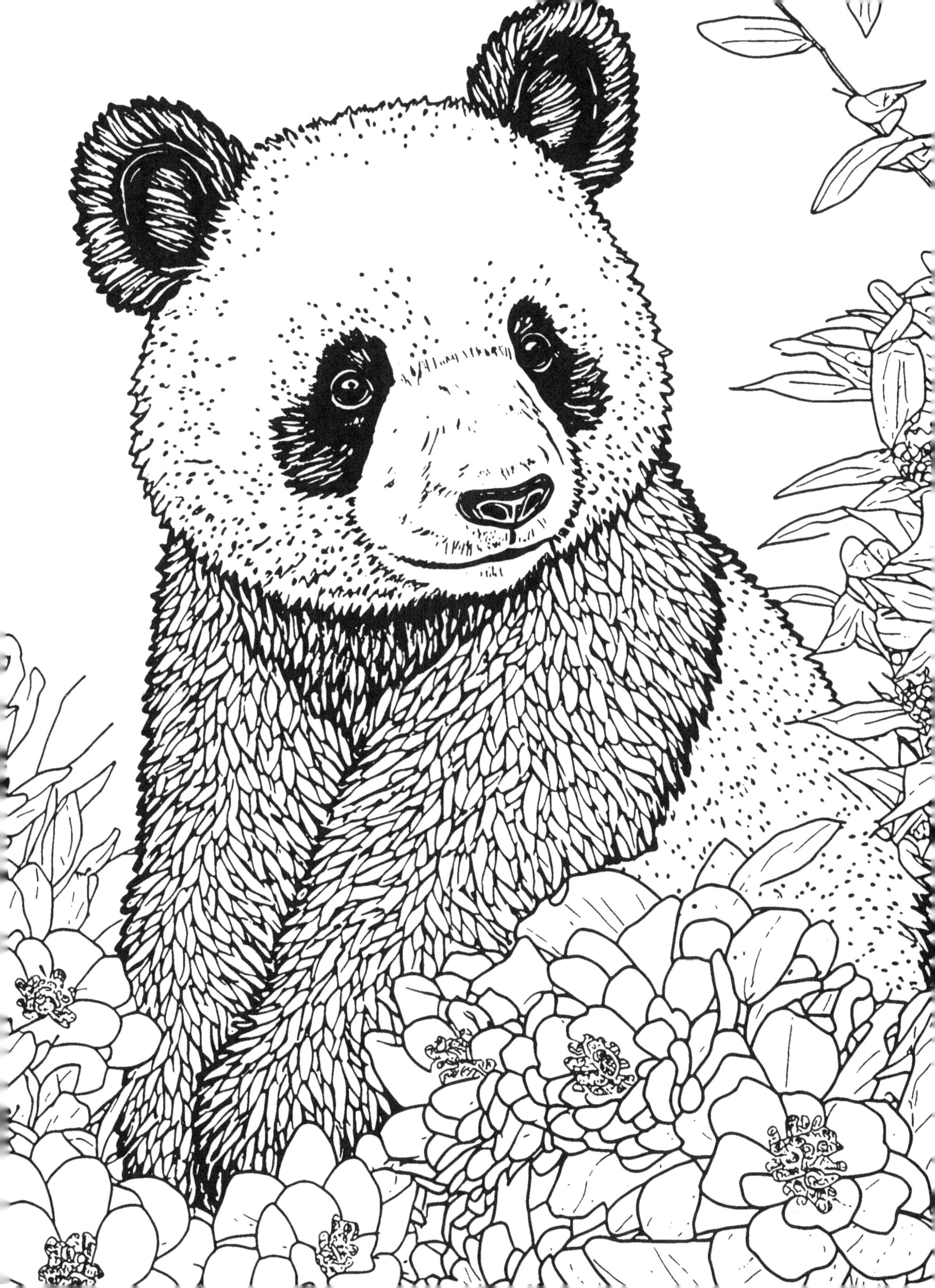

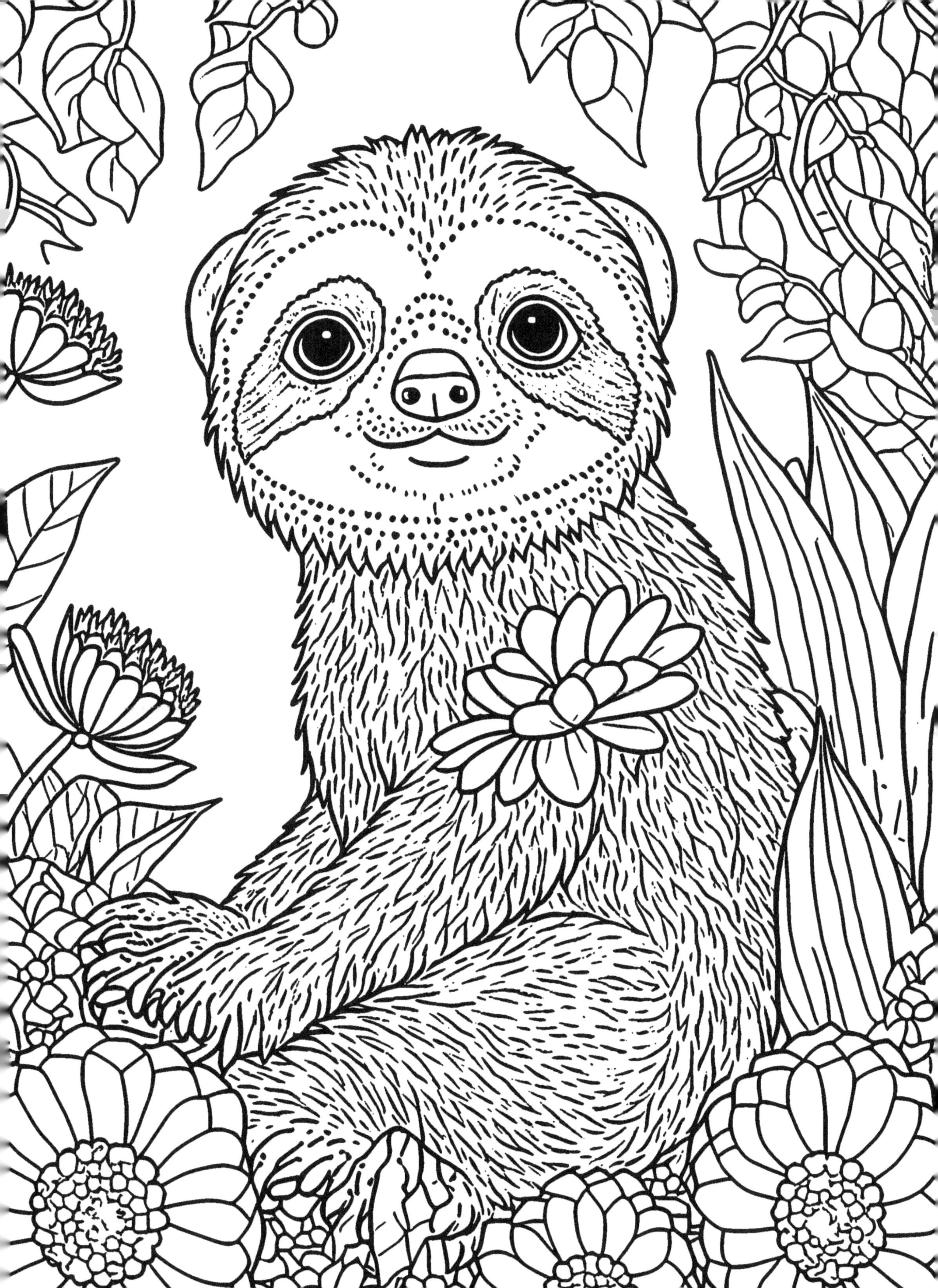

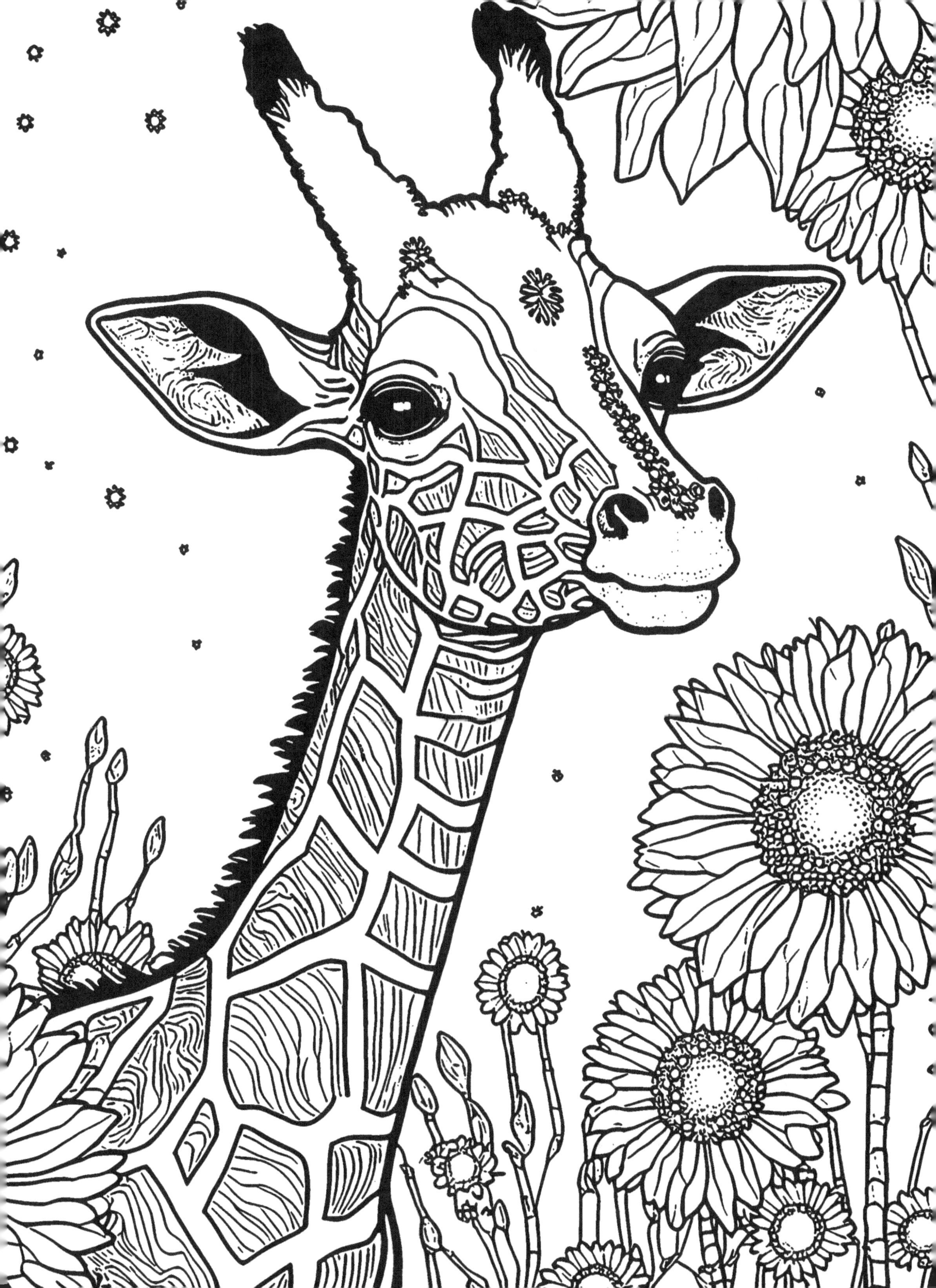

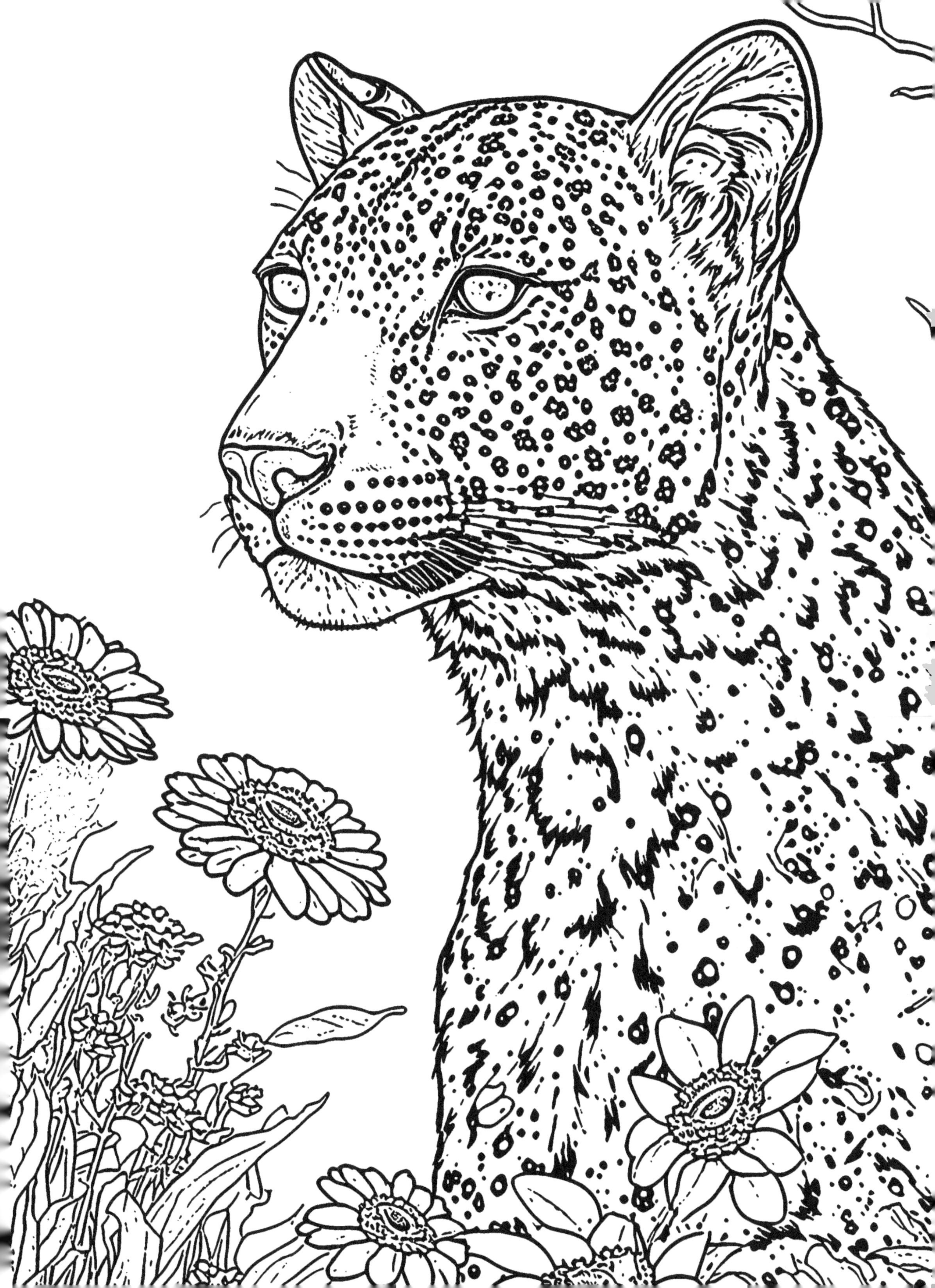

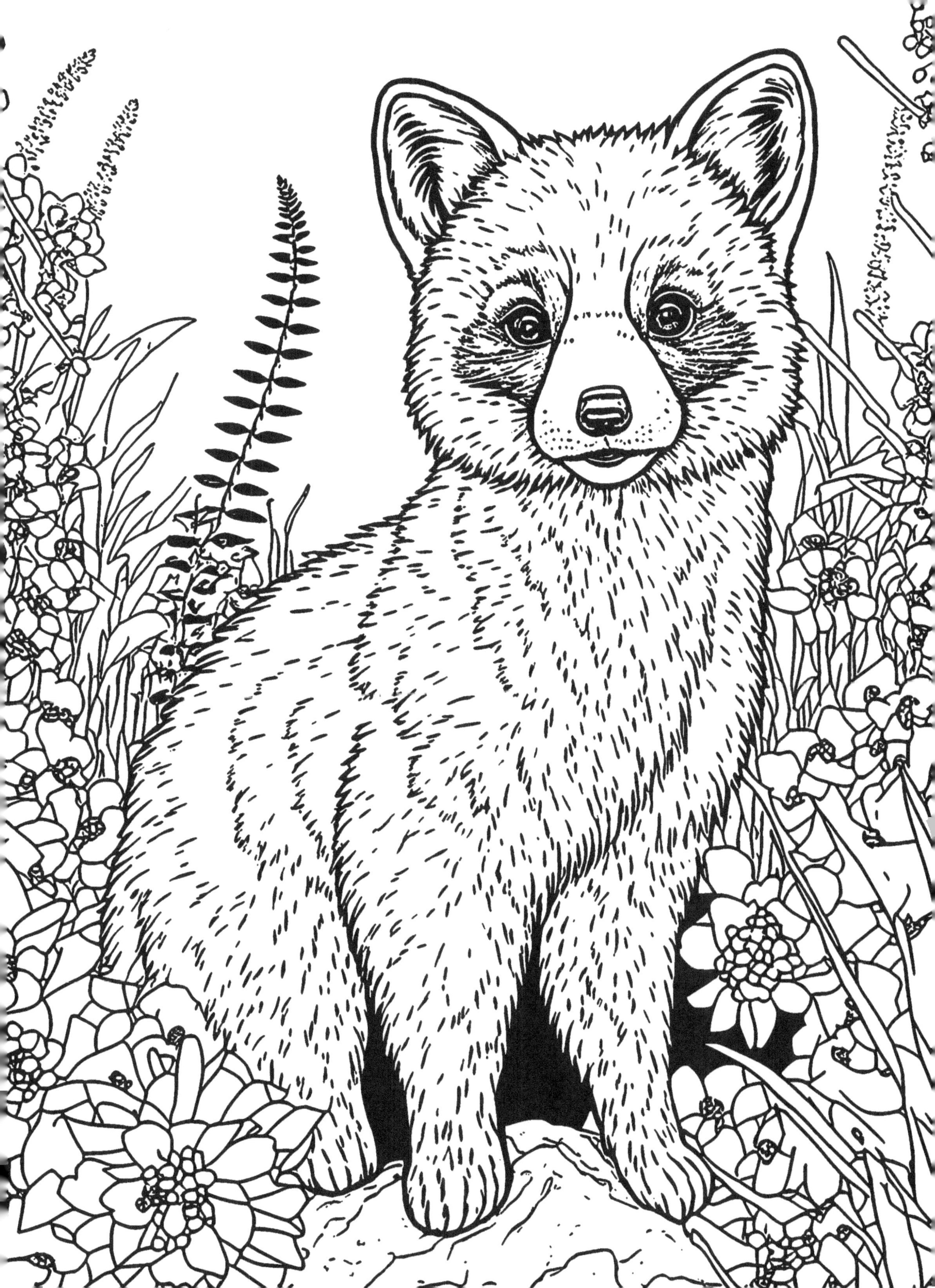

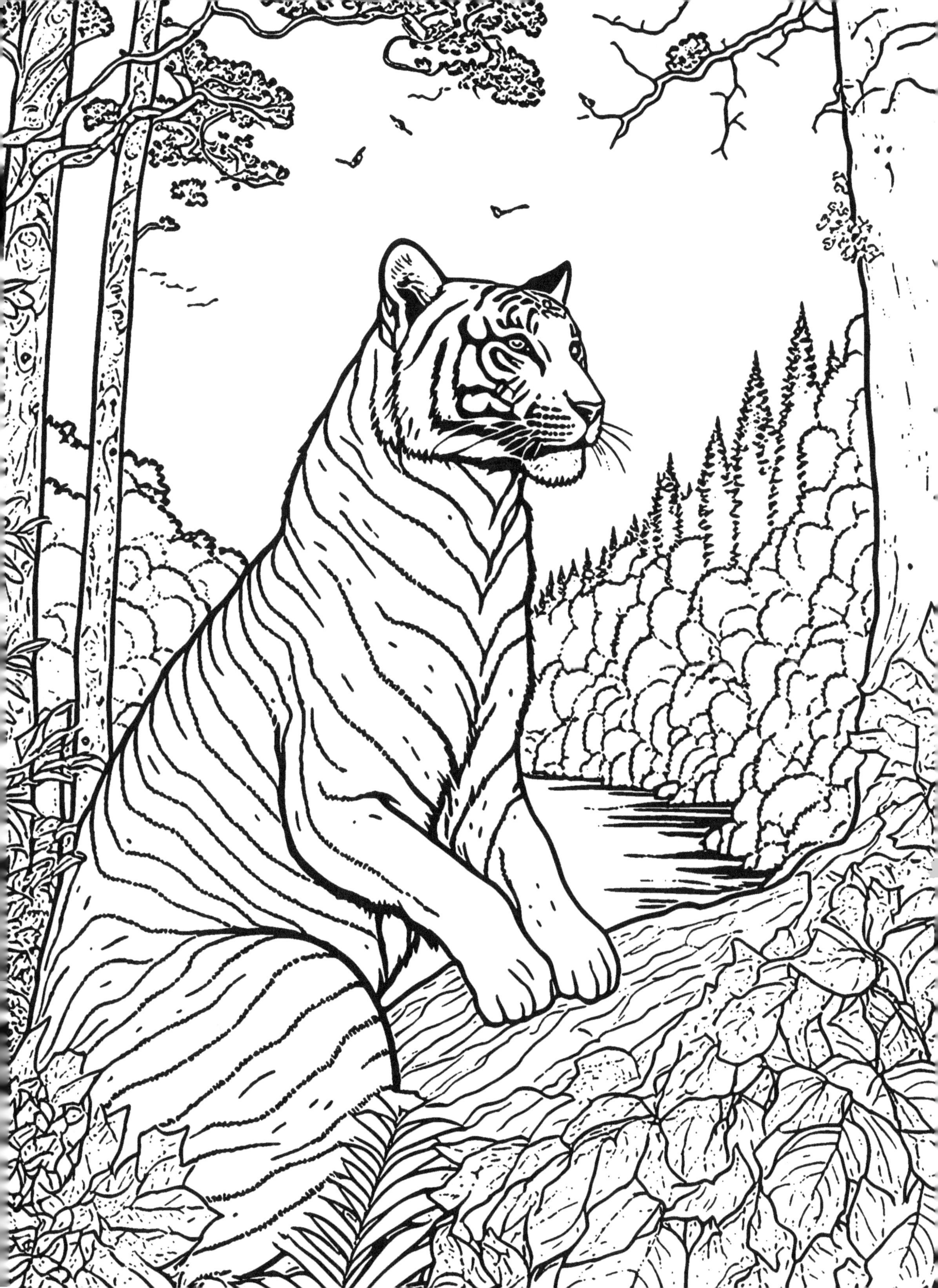

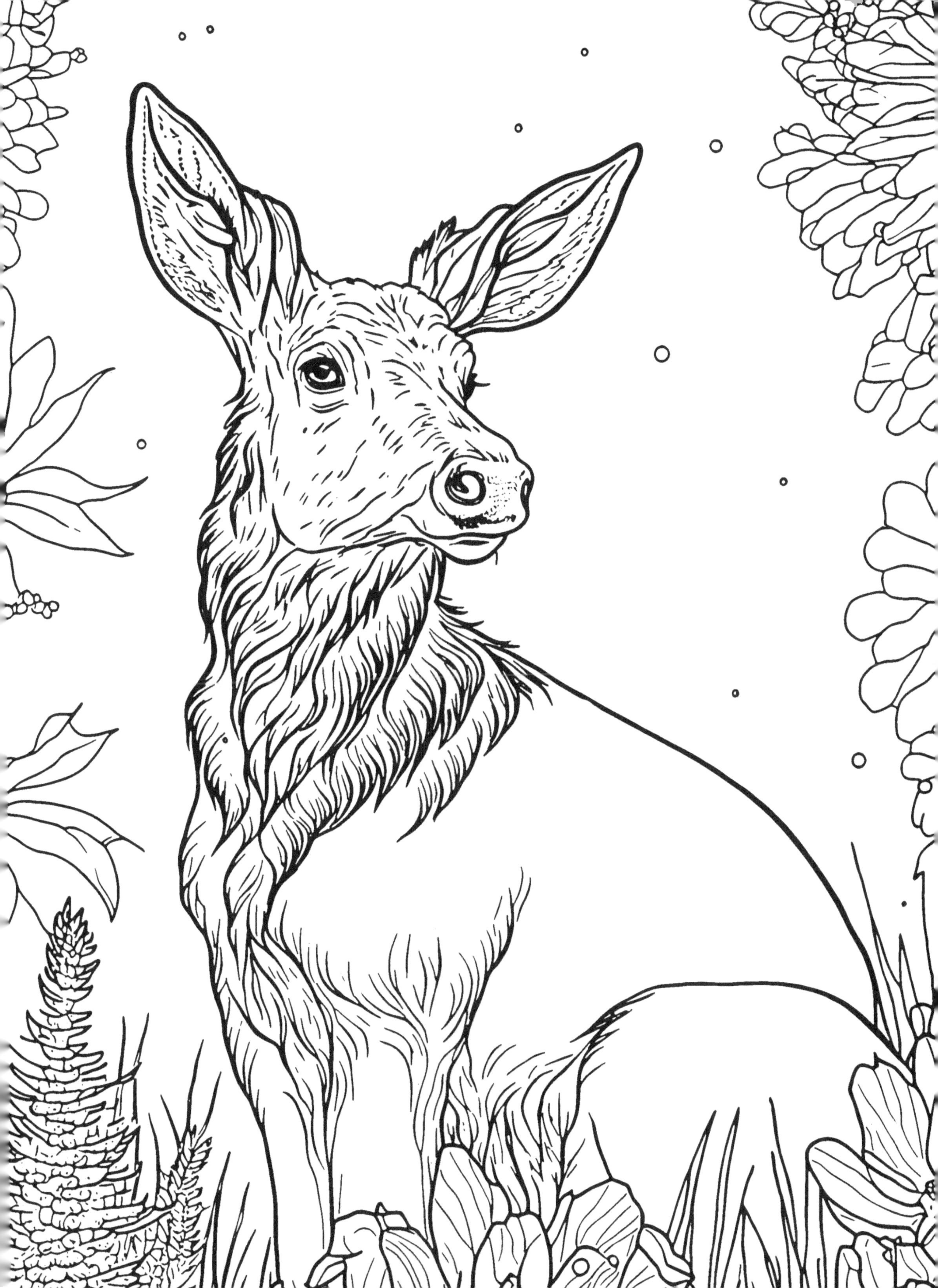

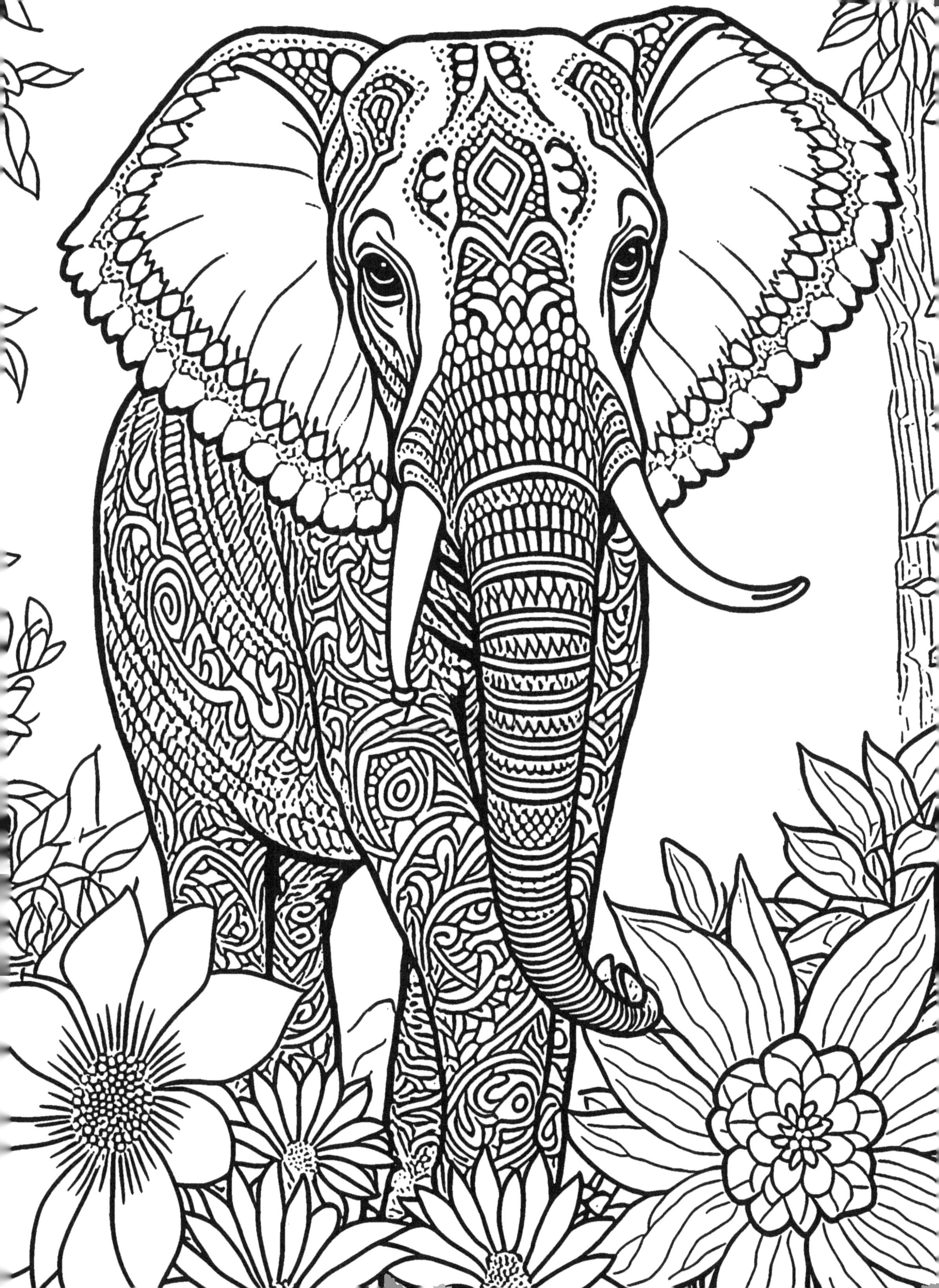

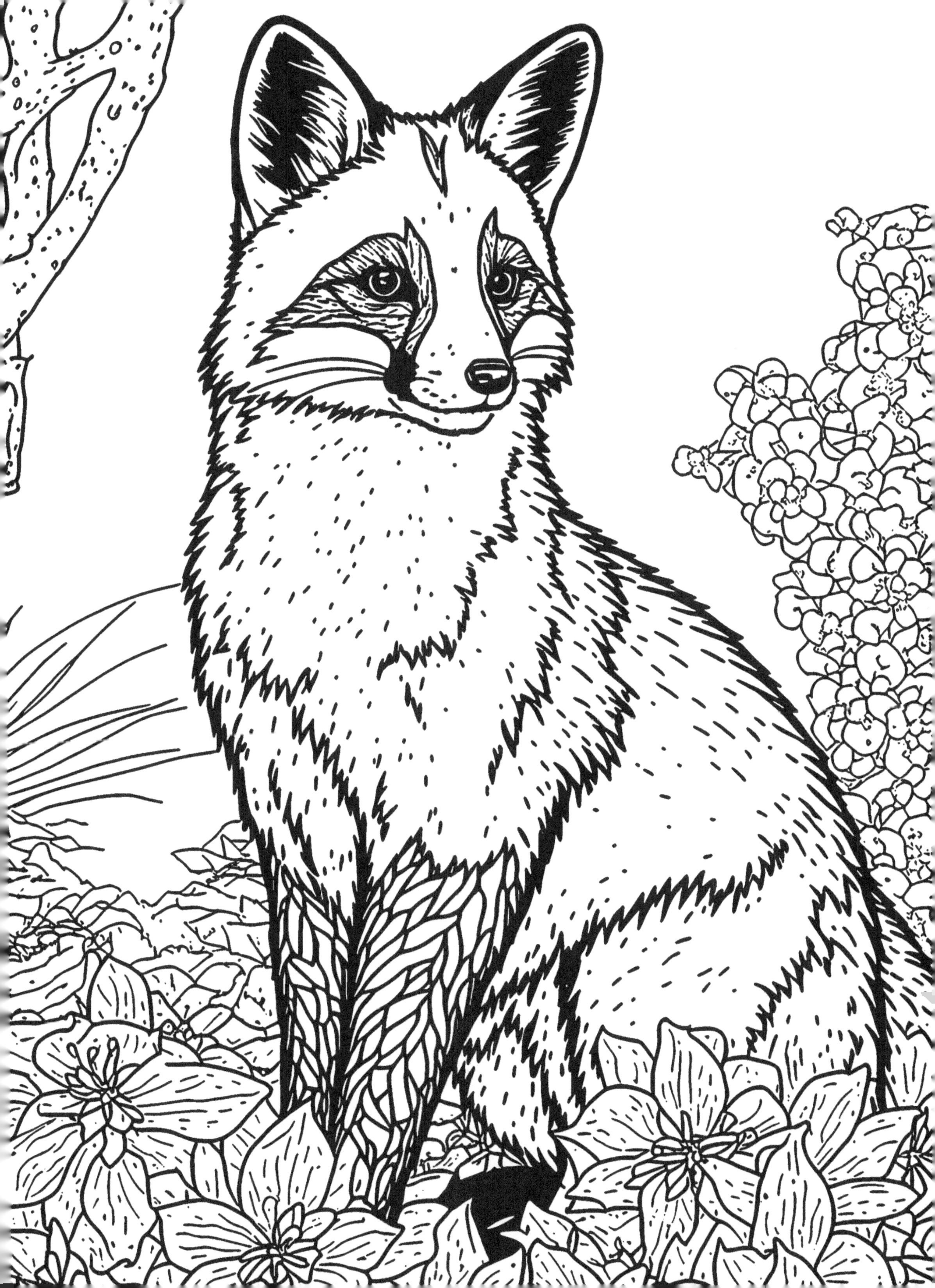

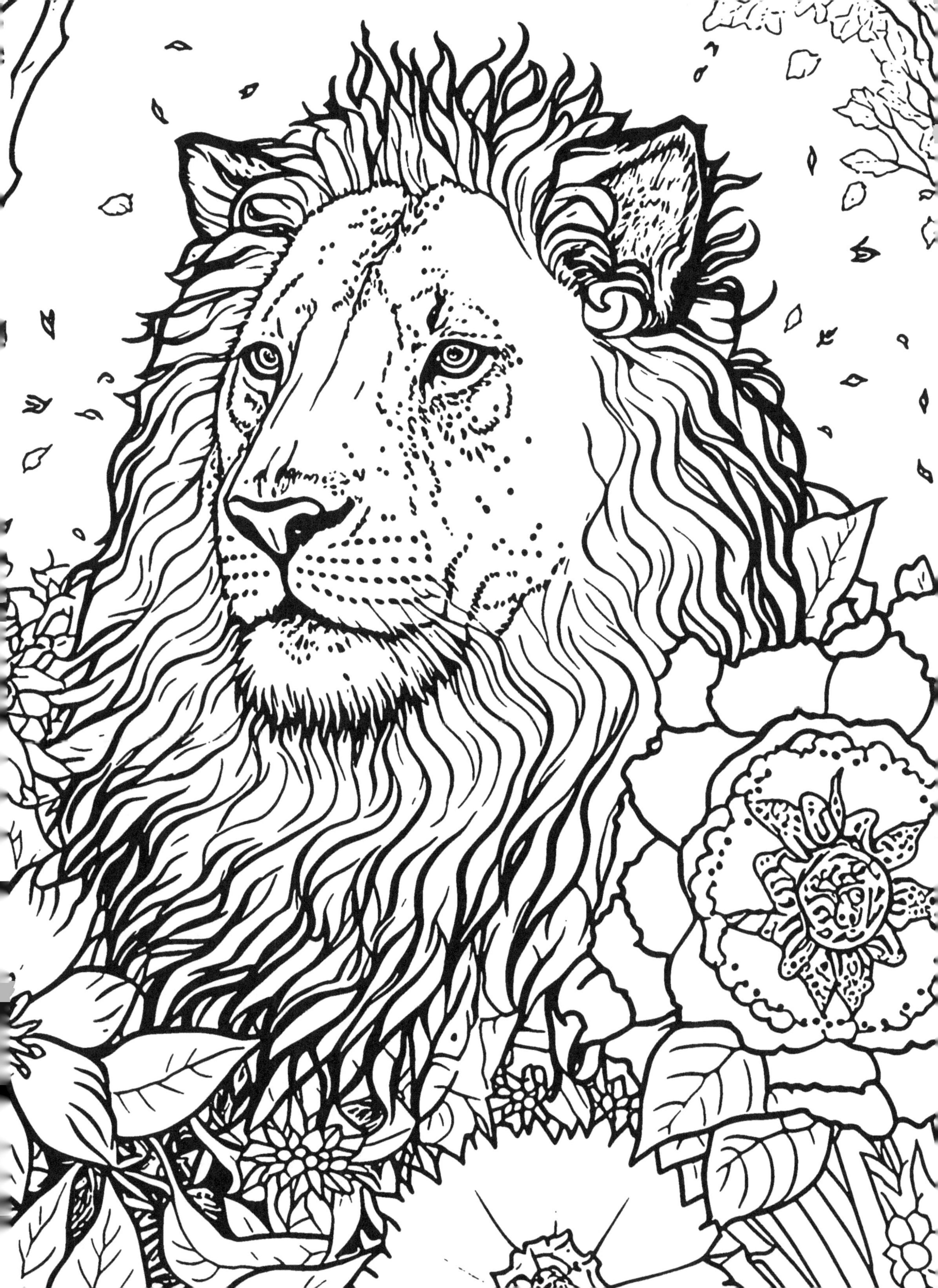

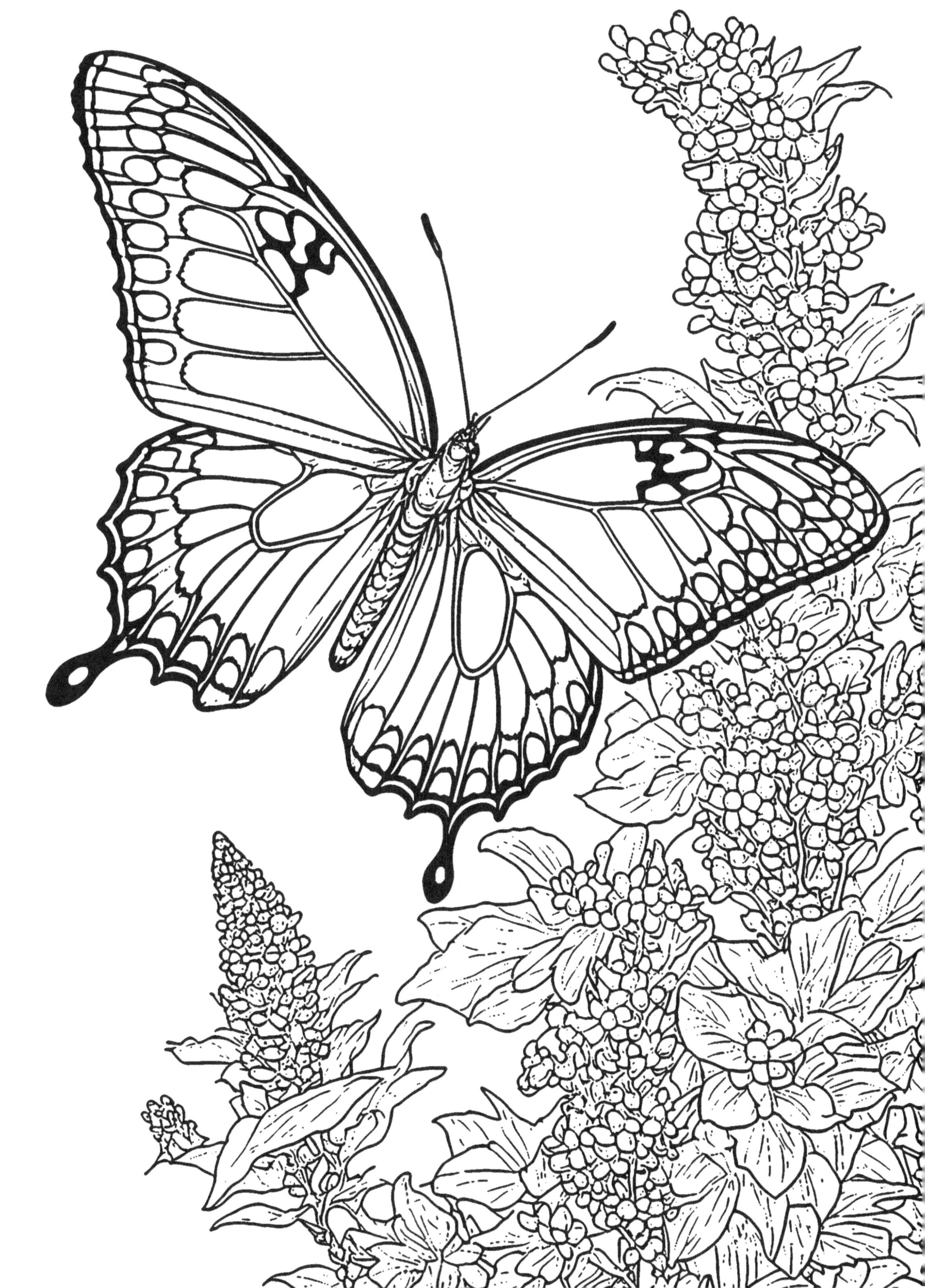

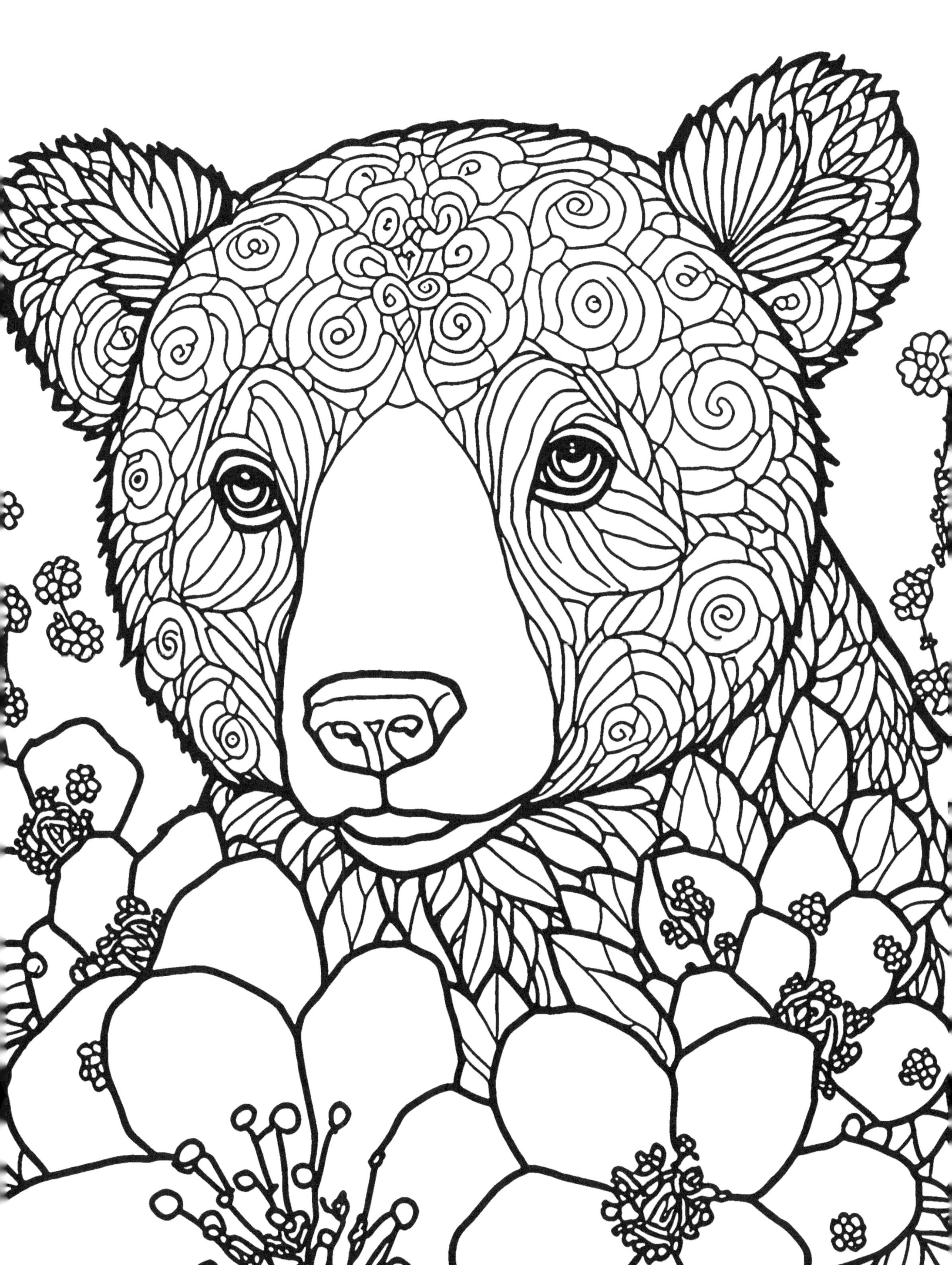